T0033872

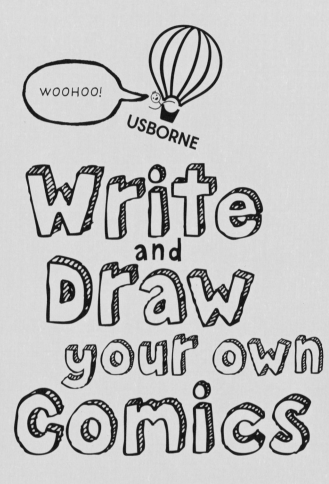

WOOHOO!

USBORNE

Write and Draw your own Comics

Write and Draw your own Comics

With amazing comic strips by...

Write your name up there.

Contents

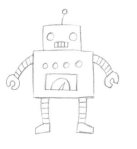

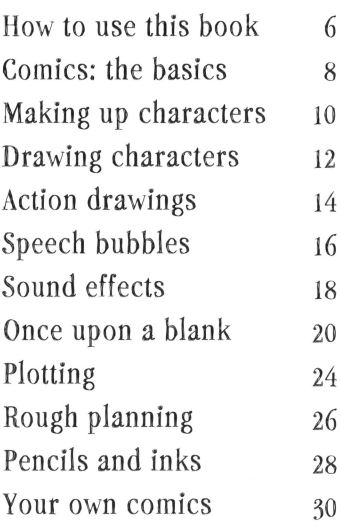

What shall I make a comic about today?

KAPOW!

Make a comic about me!

No, about me! I'm fascinating!

How to use this book

Comics use words and pictures to tell stories. This book has lots of space for you to write and draw your own comic strips, but there are also strips that have been drawn already to guide you.

There are lots of comic strips explaining important comics-making techniques.

Early in the book you'll find simple writing and drawing activities.

Later in the book you'll find comic strips giving you ideas for stories.

Your title goes here.

Your comics go here.

There are lots of tips around the edges of the pages.

At the end of the book there are even more ideas for your next comics.

Useful things

An eraser

RUB
RUB

A sharpener

A ruler

Pencils

Pens, especially fine black pens, for drawing outlines

Spare paper for sketching out ideas for your comics

A dictionary and a thesaurus might come in handy.

What's another word for "big"? Big explosion doesn't sound dramatic enough.

Thesaurus

Comics to read for inspiration

Scan the code for links to websites with activities and videos about comics, or go to usborne.com/ Quicklinks and type in the title of this book.

DICTIONARY

Comics: the basics

9

Making up characters

Before you create a comic, you need a character to star in it.

Hello!

When you're making up characters, think of questions you'd like to ask them. (Then answer them yourself.)

Who are you? Where do you live? What do you want in life?

I am whoever you want me to be, oh mighty creator.

You, just out of view

You don't have to be an amazing artist to make comics. Even stick figures make great characters.

I am awesome just the way I am.

Just adding a few details can turn a stick figure into any character you like.

I'm a queen!

I'm a ringmaster!

I'm a cat!

Your character

Turn this stick figure into a character by adding clothes and accessories. Fill in the blanks in the thought and speech bubbles, too.

One thing no one knows about me is...

....

....

Hello, my name is

....

and the thing I want most in life is

....

Giving your character a distinctive feature or two means your reader can easily tell that it's the same person all the way through your comic.

Ideas for features and accessories

Drawing characters

In comics, you can draw faces in all sorts of different ways.

Here are a few ways to draw parts of faces.

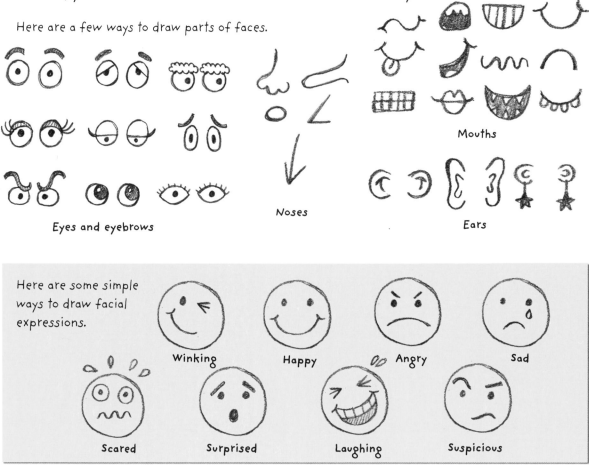

Eyes and eyebrows

Noses

Mouths

Ears

Here are some simple ways to draw facial expressions.

Winking   Happy   Angry   Sad

Scared   Surprised   Laughing   Suspicious

Now try adding expressions and features to these faces to match their names.

Suzy Brightside   Rocky Hardnut   Baddie McNasty   General Temperburst

Characters come in all shapes and sizes.
Here are a few basic body types you can use in your comics.

You could start with a stick figure and build up from there.

You could start with a rectangle or square to build up a stocky character.

For a toddler character, make it three times the height of its own head.

One head height

Grown-up human

Stocky monster

Ninja toddler

Draw your own characters with different body types. Add some details and facial expressions.

Name: ....

Name: ....

Name: ....

Action drawings

When you're making up characters, try drawing them in lots of different action poses. That helps you get a better feel for how they move around the page.

The little lines next to the figures show movement.

Some action poses to try in your comics

Shrugging

Running

Falling

Cowering in fear

Kicking a ball

SCRAMBLE!

Clinging to a cliff

Climbing

"I have a sore back" pose

Trying to pick up something heavy

100

Walking

Dancing

Slouching along sadly

Swimming

You can spread actions over several panels.
For example, here is a character jumping over an abyss.

Here are some four-legged creatures in action.

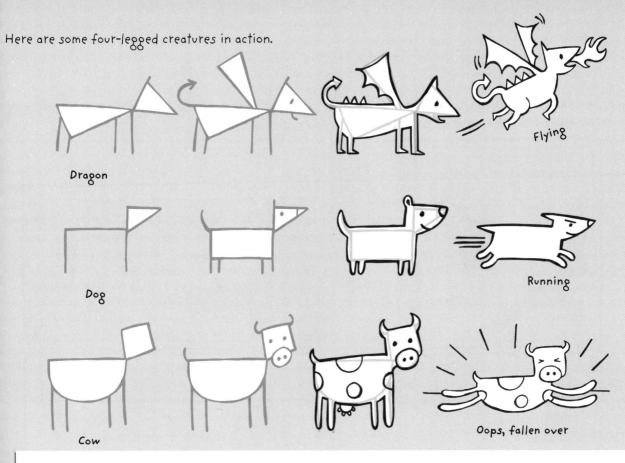

Dragon

Flying

Dog

Running

Cow

Oops, fallen over

Try drawing a four-legged creature in action.

Drawing animals doing human
activities can be funny.

15

Speech bubbles

Comics use speech bubbles – also known as speech balloons –
to show that a character is talking.

What do you think these animals are saying?
Add speech bubbles to show their conversation.

Sound effects

Noises in comics are sometimes called sound effects or SFX. The letter shapes used for SFX often reflect the sounds that are being made.

Escaping gas

Pffffft

Something disappearing

POUF !

Bigger, bolder letters make the sound seem louder.

Really loud explosion

KABOOM!

You can draw your SFX inside shapes to make them stand out more.

DING DONG!

SPLAT

This lion's roar is drawn in rough, hairy letters.

RoAAAAR!

EEeK!

Wooooo

BAM!

CRASH

FWEEEP!

Try making up your own words to describe noises.

MOO!

POW

School trip of terror

Use a felt pen to add sound effects to this spooky comic.

Once upon a blank

Long ago in a fairy tale kingdom, there was a rabbit prince.
Fill in the blanks in this four-page comic to complete his story.

What are they saying?

Give the characters names.

Once upon a time there was a rabbit prince.

Ahem, you mean a HANDSOME rabbit prince named

....

He lived in a castle with his best friend

....

One day, they were invited to the fairy king's ball. The rabbit prince had a coach, but nothing to pull it. His fairy godmother came to the rescue.

Here, this creature will pull you there in no time!

Thank you, fairy godmother!

I've never seen a beast like THAT before.

Draw a magical creature to pull the carriage.

What are the guests at the ball saying and thinking?

Is the fairy king welcoming his guests? Or complaining about the food?

What's on the fairy queen's mind? Is she enjoying herself?

Later, at the ball...

Suddenly, over the sound of the music, there was a terrible noise...

What are the dancing mice talking about?

Write a sound effect for a noise of something scary that's coming to get them.

Try saving up surprises for after a page turn. For example, on this page, there's suddenly a great big... well, that's for you to decide.

Oh no, it's...

....

Draw what the characters are running away from and add sound effects for the noise it's making.

What does she say in her spell?

Just then, the fairy godmother appeared.

Don't worry, boys, I'll save you with one of my spells.

What sound does the spell make?

BYEEE!

She's turned it into a

....

Draw what the fairy godmother has turned the scary thing from the opposite page into.

...and they all lived happily ever after. THE END.

What does the frog say about the magical transformation?

Plotting

A comic needs a plot — or story — with a beginning, a middle and an end. Here's one way to create a plot.

At the beginning, introduce a main character. For example, this goofy alien.

Which one's the brake again?

Self destruct

Then, make something happen to get the story moving.

BOOM!

ahhhhhhhhhhhhhhhhhhhh!

New York

CRASH!

Pack the middle of your story with action, excitement and problems.

HONK! HONK! HONK!

TAXI

Oh no I'm being attacked by a honkbeast!

Add some surprises and discoveries for your character to come across, too.

HONK! HONK!

Run for your liiiiiives!

Ooh what's that on the ground?

$100

As you near the end, it's time to solve your character's problems.

TAXI

$100? Hop in!

$100

Aha! I have tamed the honkbeast with this paper.

Finally, show how your character ends up. Happy? Sad?

Welcome to New York, pal!

WOO HOO!

THE END

24

Now try writing some notes for a plot of your own.

Your story's title:

_____

Beginning

Your main character is...
(Who? What?)
_____

Your story starts in...
(Place)
_____

The story gets started when...
_____

Fill in the blanks to create your plot.

Middle

One problem your character
comes up against is...
_____

_____

Your character reacts by...
_____

_____

There's a surprise when...
_____

_____

This is too exciting. I can't bear to look.

End

The character's problems are
solved when...
_____

At the end of the comic,
your character is....
(Feeling? Doing?)

My story had a happy ending... but yours doesn't have to.

Rough planning

scribble!

Once you've decided what happens in your comic, decide how many panels you want to use to tell the story. It can be helpful to write a list and sketch out a small, rough version showing what will happen in each panel.

PANEL 1: A knight is riding. A king calls to him for help.

PANEL 2: On the castle roof, the king points out a dragon.

PANEL:3 The knight fights the dragon with his lance.

PANEL 4: The dragon's fire melts the lance.

PANEL 5: The knight pushes the dragon into the river.

PANEL 6: The dragon gives up. Without its fire, it has no power.

Mini, rough comics like this are often called thumbnails.

Try drawing your own rough sketches for a comic — perhaps the story you planned on page 25. The sketches can be as messy as you like, and you don't have to use all the panels. Start by jotting down a list on rough paper of what you want to show in each panel.

Title:

Pencils and inks

It's often a good idea to draw your comics in pencil first, then pen. The first half of this comic shows the stages many comic book creators go through.

Pictures and speech bubbles drawn in pencil

Black ink added over pencils

Pencil lines erased

Foreground (the front of the picture) filled in

Background filled in and shading added

Black ink added over the words in speech bubbles

Go over the rest of this strip in black pen. Then fill in the foreground and background in pencils or pens.

Your own comics

Now it's over to you. Fill the rest of the book with your own comics. Add the titles of your comics here as you go along.

(Mix and match comic, pages 33–37)

(Good day, bad day, pages 39–43)

(Superheroes vs robots, pages 46–49)

(Dinos in danger, pages 52–55)

(Pirates and treasure, pages 58–61)

You'll find lots of story ideas and drawing tips around the edges of the pages in case you need any help.

(Tiny adventure, pages 63-67)

(Secret agents, pages 69-73)

(Fantasy quest, pages 75-79)

(How to be a cat, pages 81-85)

(Time travel, pages 87-91)

Mix and match comic

Choose from these characters and places to create a comic. There are suggestions for events and hints along the way to help you.

Characters

Astronaut on the run from the space police

Pirate mermaid

Bear who's obsessed with watching TV

Excitable robot

Talking skull with a bad attitude

Queen bee

Grumpy circus performer

Mysterious woman on horseback

Annoying little brother or sister

Places

An underground city

Magical library

An alien planet

A park

A supermarket

A spooky forest full of eyes

Fairyland

Ancient Egypt

Now start your comic. ➡

What's your title?

Pick a main character and a place for your story to start.

Show your character going about her or his daily life. You could divide up the panels if you like.

Drawing conversations

Single speaker

Speaker and listener

Two speakers. The first speaker's bubble is higher than the second speaker's.

Continued ▶

A new character arrives. Pick one from the page opposite.
What do the two characters say to one another?

Things take a turn for the worse. Pick an event that makes things more difficult for the characters.

Events

A character...

...gets kidnapped.
...is sucked through a portal into another dimension.
...goes to a new school.
...goes on a journey.
...learns to fly.
...meets her or his worst enemy.
...eats or drinks something forbidden.
...flies through an asteroid field.
...climbs a mysterious flight of stairs.
...fights a duel.

Your main character finds an object that helps to make things better.

Objects

 Key   Crown   Kitten   Ray gun   Rotten banana   Magic potion   Letter   Screwdriver

Your characters go somewhere new.
Pick a place and draw them arriving.

Hold on tight!

The space police are catching up!

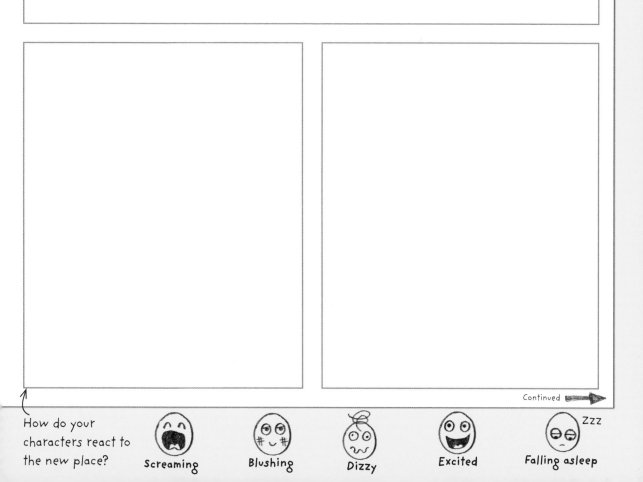

Continued ➡

How do your characters react to the new place?

Screaming   Blushing   Dizzy   Excited   Falling asleep   Zzz

Something unexpected happens.
(Pick another event.)

To another
dimension

Nooooooo!

Using a huge panel can make a dramatic event seem even more
important. You can also show lots of action happening at once.

Something happens to complicate your main character's life.  *I am your father.*

What does your character do about it?

The end.

(Or is it?)

Endings

Big battle Fire the cannons! Party Goodbye To be continued... YOU?!

Good day, bad day

Start your comic on the next page. ➡

Start with either a bad or a good thing happening. Your day could take you anywhere in the world (or out of it).

You could make each good or bad thing last for a couple of panels.

Vary the scale of the pictures in your panels.

Close up

Oh no!

From a distance

Oh no!

08.00

Continued ➡

SCHOOL

The school has vanished!

Who's eaten my toast?

AIEEEE!

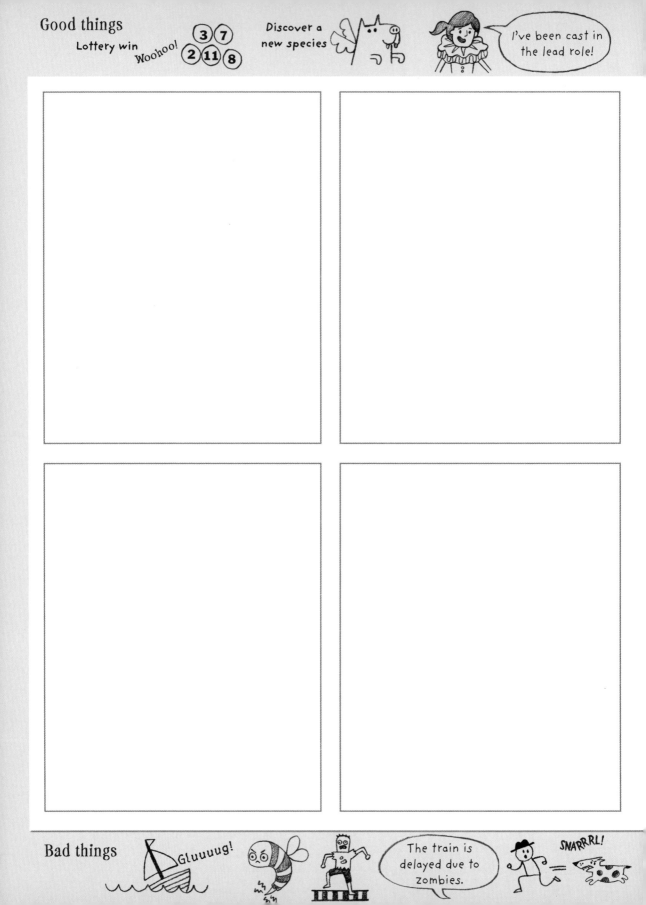

Good things

Lottery win Woohoo! ③⑦②⑪⑧

Discover a new species

I've been cast in the lead role!

Bad things

Gluuuug!

The train is delayed due to zombies.

SNARRRL!

You could use some captions like these to show time passing.

Later...

Meanwhile...

Seconds later...

After lunch...

Some time later...

That evening...

Continued

Good things

GOAL!

Shiny limo

Your chauffeur is here.

I have good news!

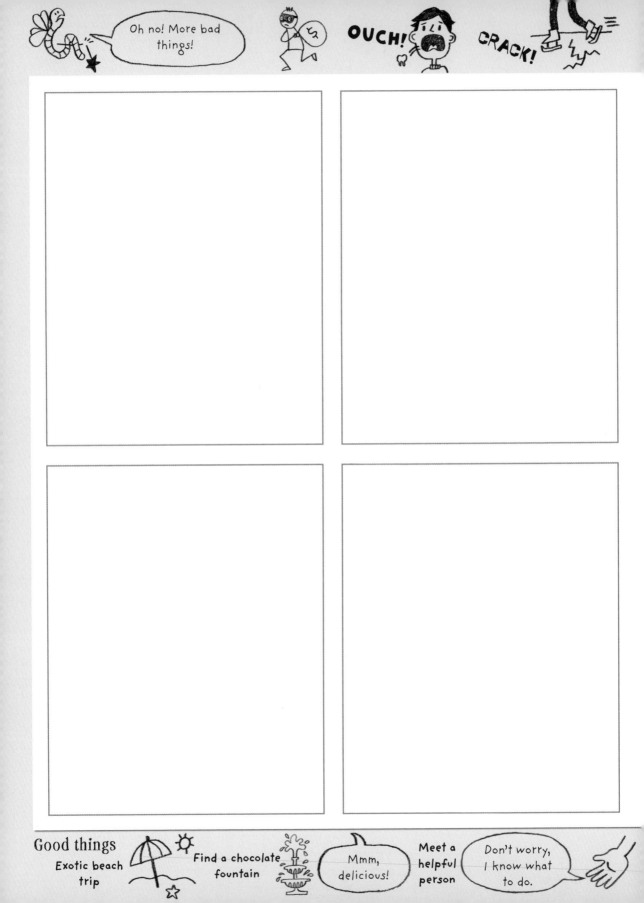

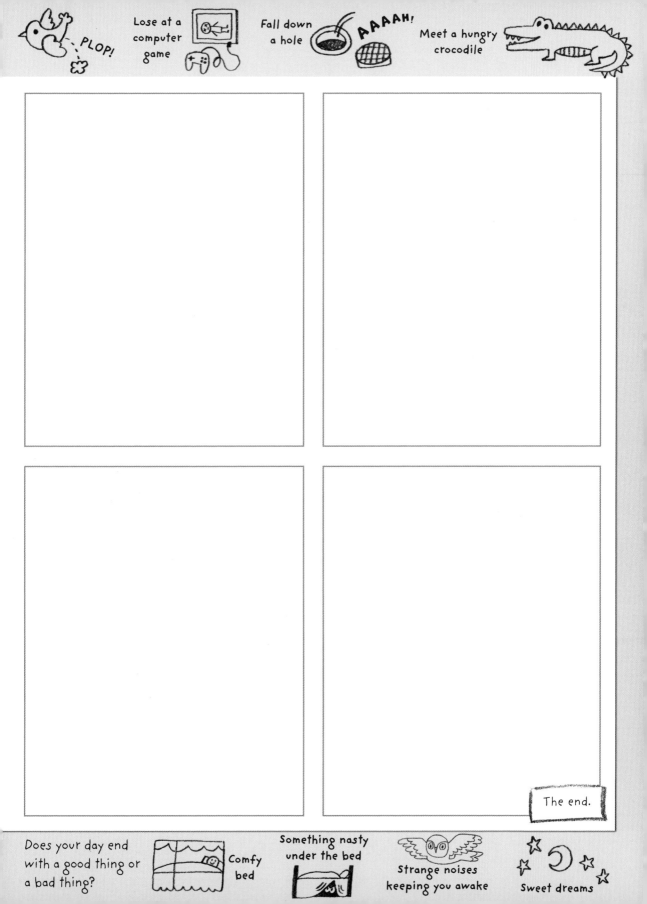

PLOP!

Lose at a computer game

Fall down a hole

AAAAH!

Meet a hungry crocodile

The end.

Does your day end with a good thing or a bad thing?

Comfy bed

Something nasty under the bed

Strange noises keeping you awake

Sweet dreams

Superheroes vs robots

In a superhero story, the bad guys have to be extra-powerful, or it would be too easy for your hero to beat them.

Give your superhero a weakness too — perhaps there's something your character is super-allergic to or afraid of.

Before you start...

What's your hero like? Fill in this card.

NAME ---------------------------------

POWERS -------------------------------

WEAKNESSES ---------------------------

PERSONALITY --------------------------

Draw your superhero here.

Create a superhero costume that matches your character's name and personality. I'm Shadow Tabby, by the way.

Cat mask

Cat logo

Boots with stripes like a tabby cat

You could include some of these things in your costume design.

Cape

Mask

Boots and gloves

Superhero logo

Start your comic on the next page. ➡

Step-by-step killer robot

You could add different details, such as an evil logo.

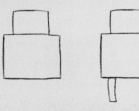

What's your title?

Draw some killer robots rampaging through a city. Then draw your hero arriving in the next panel.

In this big panel, show how your superhero attacks the robots.

You can make your characters look as though they're moving by using lines like these.

Flying
WHOOSH!

Punching
SMACK!

Running super-fast
ZOOOM!

Falling
Aaaaaaaa!

Here's a simple way to draw the buildings in the background.

Continued ➤

Does anyone come to help your superhero?

Mayor of Metrotown

WOO-WOO-WOO!!

Innocent bystander

Sidekick

Giant killer robots don't make themselves... who do you think is in control of these metal menaces?

Evil alien lord?

Fiendish scientist?

A mysterious supervillain?

Show your hero facing his or her enemy. What does the villain want?

Revenge?

MWAHAHA!

To take over the world?

To shrink superheroes

How does your hero defeat the evil villain and the killer robots?

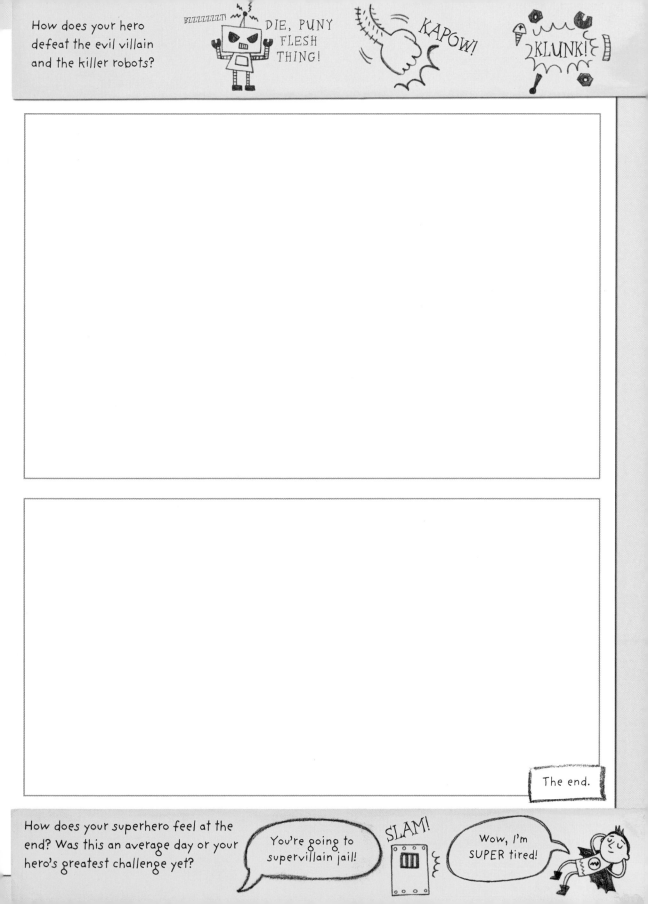

BZZZZZZZZT! DIE, PUNY FLESH THING!

KAPOW!

KLUNK!

The end.

How does your superhero feel at the end? Was this an average day or your hero's greatest challenge yet?

You're going to supervillain jail!

SLAM!

Wow, I'm SUPER tired!

Dinos in danger

The land of the dinosaurs is full of deadly perils... which is bad for the dinosaurs, but good for your imagination.

Flaming meteors

I'm glad I'm not a dinosaur!

Carnivorous dinosaurs

Erupting volcanoes

Make up some dinosaur characters and put them in danger.

Help meee!

Nooooo!

DANGER

Here are some ideas for dinosaurs you could use in your comic. What are their personalities like?

I could be a vicious killer.

But then again, maybe I'm just a great big teddy bear with tiny arms.

Am I cheerful? Nervous? Brave? Talkative? Really, really annoying?

Everyone can see that I'm enormous, but am I good or evil? Brainy or a little slow?

I'm a prehistoric wasp!

BZZZZ!

Am I helpful or harmful? Friend or foe?

Do your dinosaurs work as a team? Do they all like one another? Are some enemies?

Drawing dinos

Flying dinosaur

Large vegetarian dinosaur

Carnivorous T-rex

Draw your dino character here in an action pose.

Name: ....

Personality: ....

....

Shadow of a big dinosaur

Try drawing a large dinosaur from below to make it look even bigger.

Make a tiny dinosaur appear even smaller by drawing it from above.

Start your dino comic on the next page.

What's your title? →

Dino dangers

Volcanoes

scREEch!

Rushing, rocky river

Giant insects

Places COOL CAVE Drip! DrOp! Drip! UNDERGROUND LAKE TOWERING MOUNTAIN

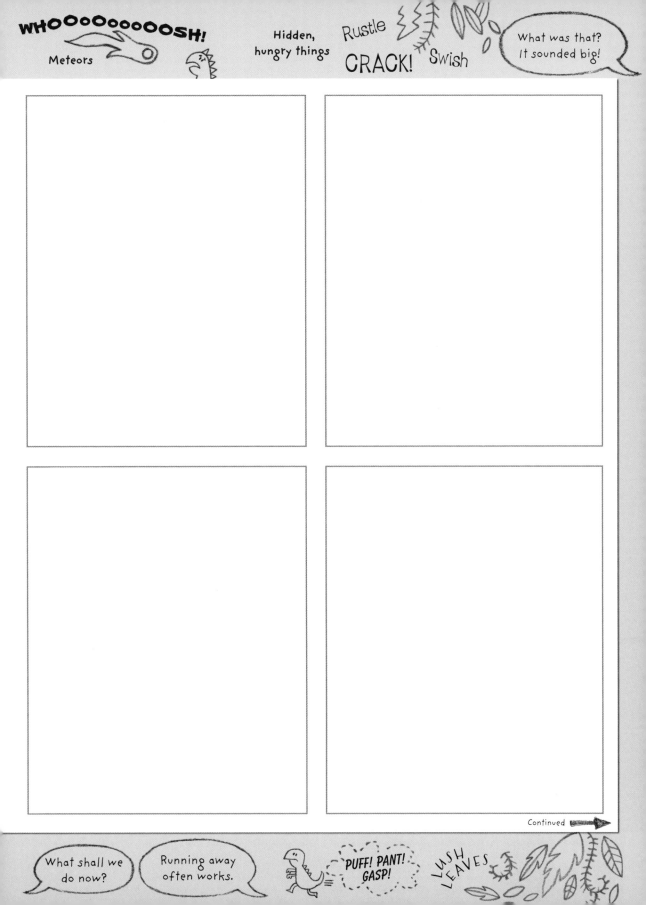

Continued ➡

CHOMP! More dino dangers

Dino-hunting
Time Tourists

Well, I've never
seen one of
THOSE before.

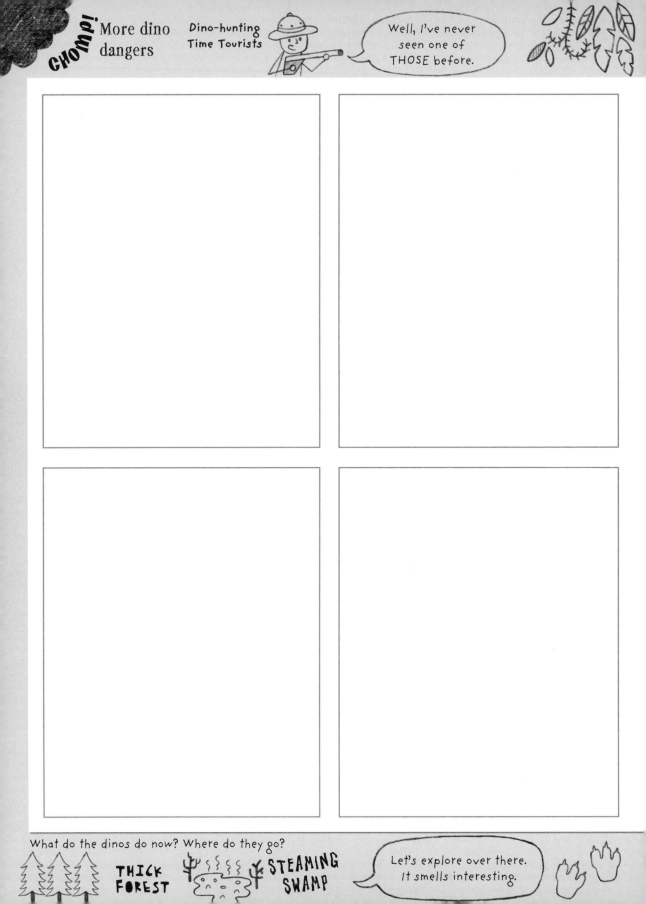

What do the dinos do now? Where do they go?

THICK
FOREST

STEAMING
SWAMP

Let's explore over there.
It smells interesting.

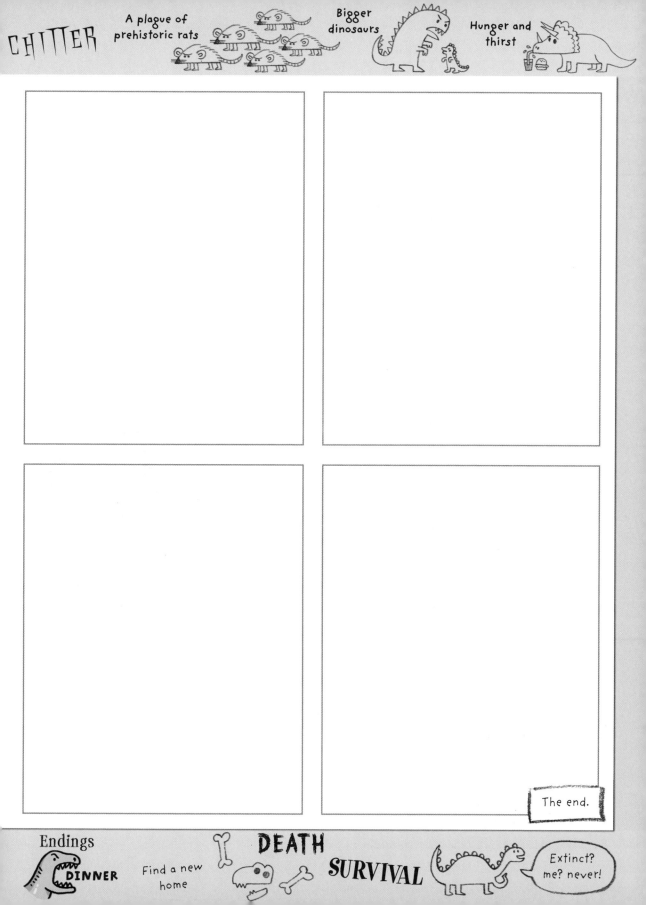

The end.

Endings

DINNER

Find a new home

DEATH

SURVIVAL

Extinct? me? never!

Pirates and treasure

Ahoy there, matey. It be time to make a pirate comic.

Design a pirate

Add a face, hands (or tentacles) and legs (or perhaps a tail) to create your own pirate character.

Is your pirate the captain of a ship? A cabin boy or girl? The ship's cook? A sea monster?

Step-by-step pirate ship

What is your pirate ship's name?

....

Think up some places your pirates could sail to and add them to this map.

Add an X to mark the spot where the treasure is buried.

Treasure island

Mermaid cove

The sea of lost souls

Add some dangers they might face along the way.

Sharks

Sharp rocks

Terrible storms

Sea monsters

Ghostly pirate ships

Start your pirate comic on the next page. ➡

AHOY THERE!

What's your title?

Lily-livered

Scurvy sea dog

Davy Jones's Locker

Where does your pirate set sail from?

Who's your pirate's crew? Here are some ideas for pirates.

Timmy Tinybones

Captain Plankwalk

Mad Lizzie Tarsniff

Events

Man overboard!

EATEN

Sea battle with enemy pirates

ATTACK!

Stock up on supplies

58

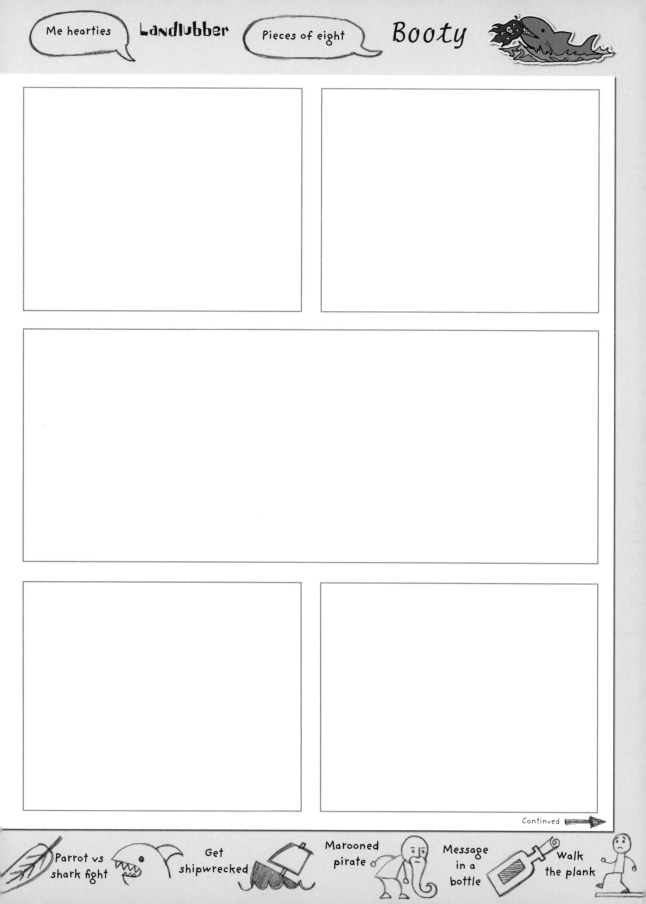

Continued ➤

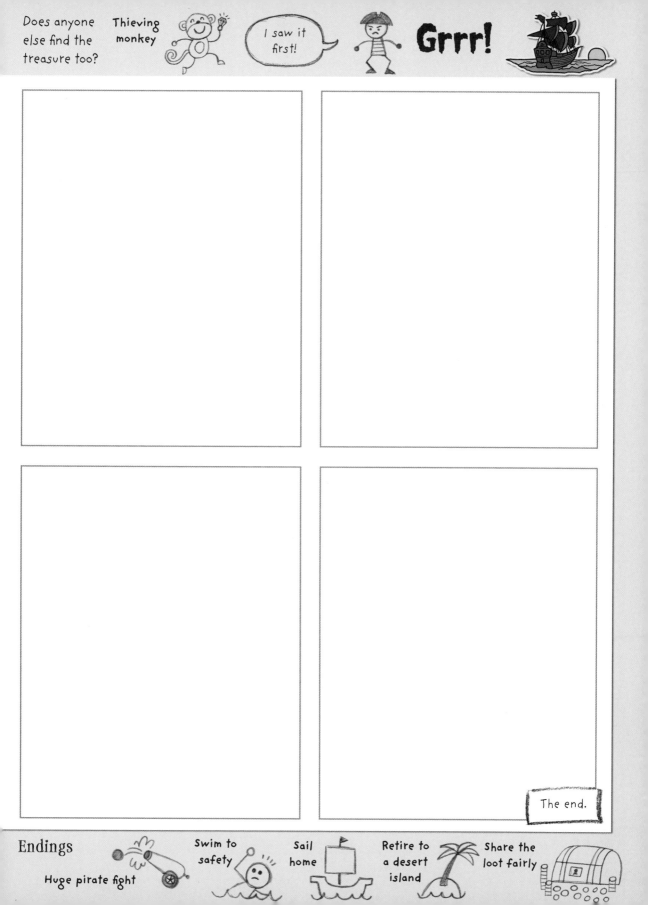

Does anyone else find the treasure too?

Thieving monkey

I saw it first!

Grrr!

The end.

Endings

Huge pirate fight

Swim to safety

Sail home

Retire to a desert island

Share the loot fairly

Tiny adventure

Imagine waking up one morning to find you'd shrunk. A lot.

Eep!

thumb

To a tiny person, the world would seem like a completely different — and more dangerous — place.

A simple walk in the park would become a perilous jungle trek.

That bee's as big as a dog! And that snail's as big as I am!

What would you do? Where would you go? How would you survive?

Continued ▶

Tiny person dangers

Getting flushed down the drain

Hunger

I can't reach the fridge. Maybe I can find some crumbs?

Pets

SWIPE!

Mini hiding places

Continued ➡

What's your title?

Where do you wake up? Where do you go next?

If you were tiny, sounds would seem louder, so you could use big dramatic SFX letters for what would usually be quiet sounds.

BLAM!

↖ Someone shutting a drawer, maybe.

Finally, a door I have a hope of opening. Maybe I can hurl myself through it?

Getting around

Don't look down, don't look down...

Physical activities

Sprint =    Clamber   Slide

When you're tiny, you have to improvise...   Bed   Hat (made from an acorn)   Cup

As your story reaches its climax, what if...

...you shrank even more?

Germ

...you grew to a giant size?

The end.

Ending ideas

You become ruler of the insects in the park.

You make a snug home in your sock drawer.

You go back to normal and write a comic about your experiences.

Secret agents

Spies operate in a mysterious, shadowy world.

Welcome, agent. I've been expecting you.

They follow secret orders.

Your next mission is to ▮▮▮▮▮▮ and ▮▮▮▮▮ in ▮▮▮.

Spies have to face terrifying dangers.

Give me the code or I'll let go!

But on the plus side, they do get to play with fun gadgets.

ERK!

Activate jet pack. Byeeee!

Fill in this top secret ID card for your spy character.

Is this a government agency such as MI6 or the CIA? A private company? Aliens?

?

Real name...

Cover identity...

Employer...

Current mission..

....

CLASSIFIED

Start your spy comic on the next page.

Title?

Flick

BURN AFTER READING

Mission ideas

Retrieve a top secret computer file from an enemy base.

Rescue a hostage.

Stop a bomb from going off.

This could be your spy's first mission. Perhaps it's a test to see if she or he will make a good spy?

Continued ➡

Spy words

Panel ideas

 **CLASSIFIED**

Mystery assailant

ASSASSIN

For Your Eyes Only

You could just draw a speech bubble against a black background for a panel in darkness.

To show a speaker without revealing her or his identity, try this.

You could draw some panels from the character's point of view, as though looking through their eyes... or their binoculars.

Gadgets and kit

 Bug (for listening in to conversations)

 Parachute

 Disguise

 Fake passport

 Robot surveillance bee

Handler
(a spy's
boss)

Tailing (following
enemies)

cryptography
(code making and breaking)

Biological weapon

Password

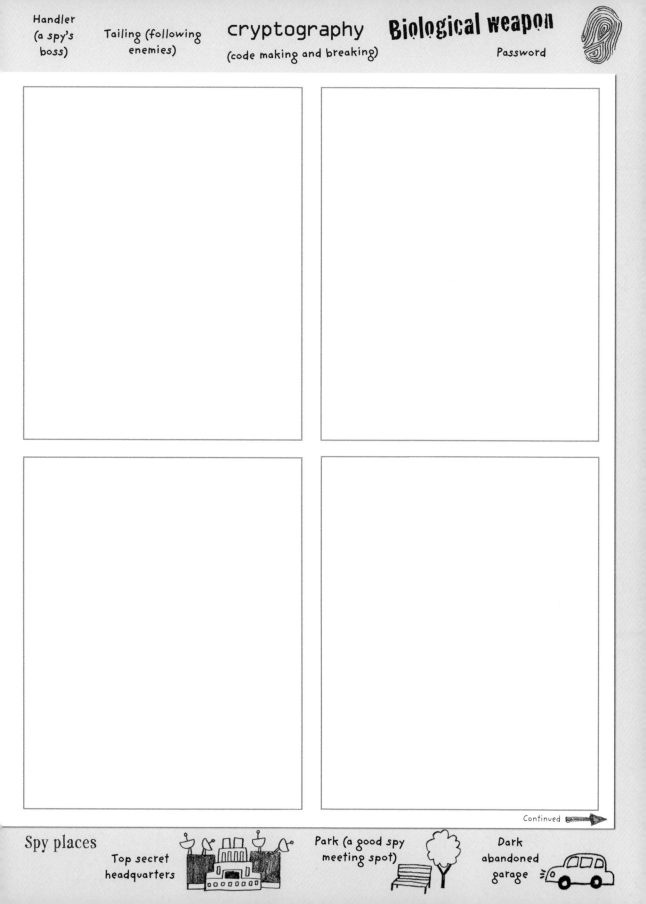

Continued

Spy places

Top secret
headquarters

Park (a good spy
meeting spot)

Dark
abandoned
garage

ACCESS DENIED

TAKA-TAKA-TAKA

BIP
BEEP

Spy problems

Gadget malfunction

Traitors and
double agents

I trusted
you!

Car chase

Explosive device

Cut the blue
wire... no, the
red one!

INTRUDER
ALERT

Wrong password

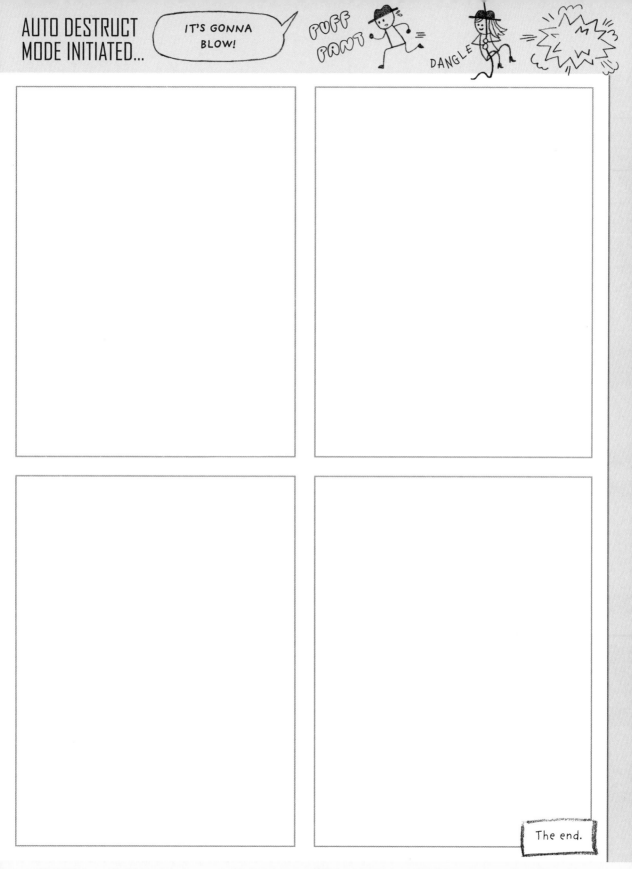

Fantasy quest

When a hero goes on a journey to seek something important, it is often called a quest.

During quests, heroes face obstacles that they must overcome. Obstacles such as this big spiny monster, for example.

I seek the enchanted Pants of Asgaroth!

The Pants are mine, puny child!

Correction. They WERE yours.

Some fantasy characters you could use

Genie from a magic lamp

Wise old man

Tough unicorn

Orphaned goblin

I will help you fight your enemies.

SNIFF!

SOB!

Will you be my friend?

Evil overlord

MWAHAHAHA!

Brave dwarf

Weird monster

Sea serpent

What is your title, mortal?

Who or what is your questing hero and what is she or he seeking?

Goblin

Human

Dwarf

Sea serpent
(Who says sea serpents can't be heroes?)

Continued ➤

Quest objects

Magic shield that makes you super-strong

Fountain of eternal youth

Sacred chalice of the gods

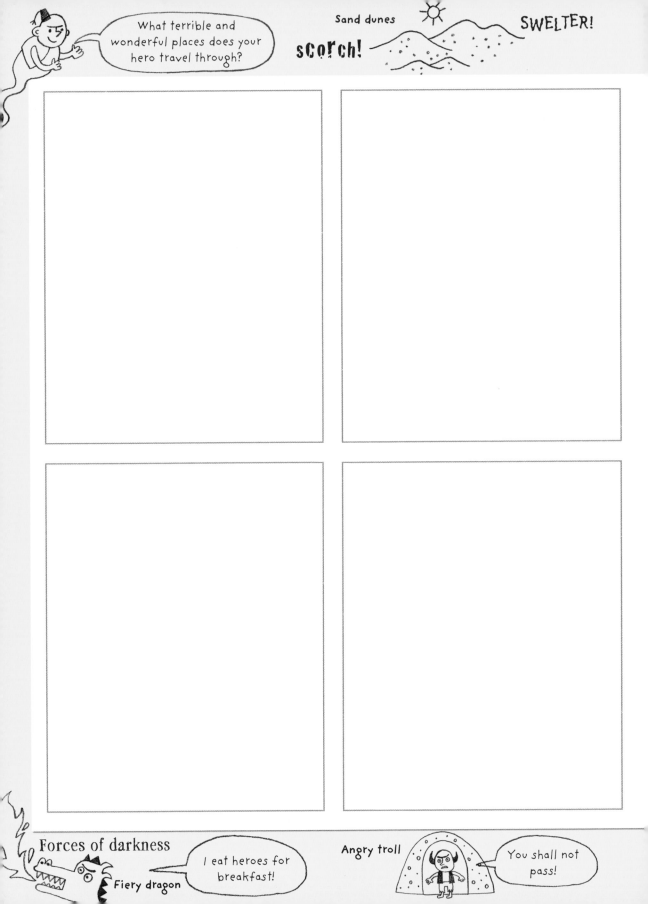

Is it safe to go in here?

Rushing river

Snowy mountains

Deep, dark caves

Tangled forest

Continued ➡

SNARL!

Giant, poisonous spider

SSSSSSSSSS!

Goblin king

Off with their heads! I could use a snack.

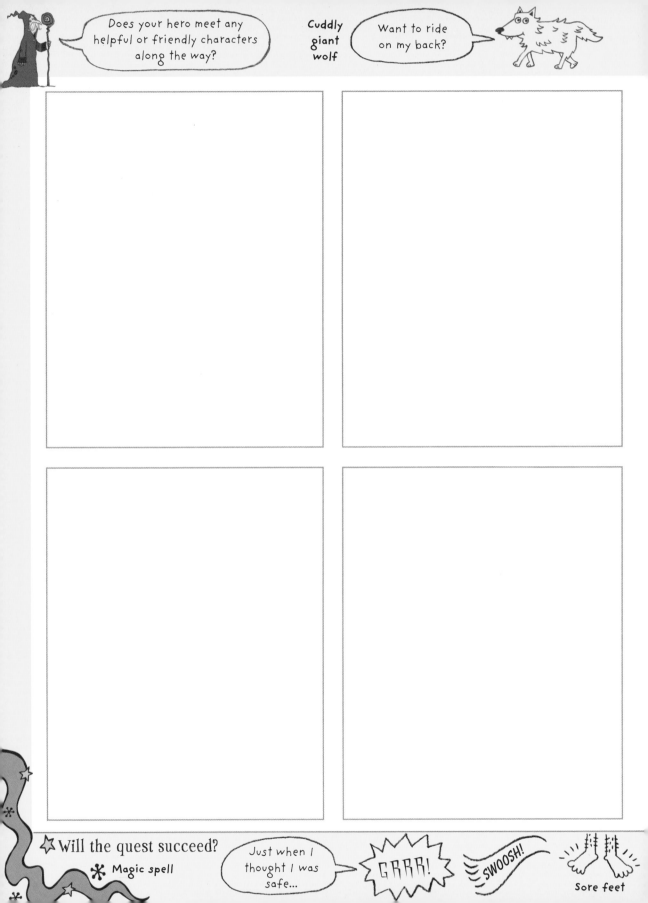

Does your hero meet any helpful or friendly characters along the way?

Cuddly giant wolf

Want to ride on my back?

Will the quest succeed?

Magic spell

Just when I thought I was safe...

GRRR!

SWOOSH!

Sore feet

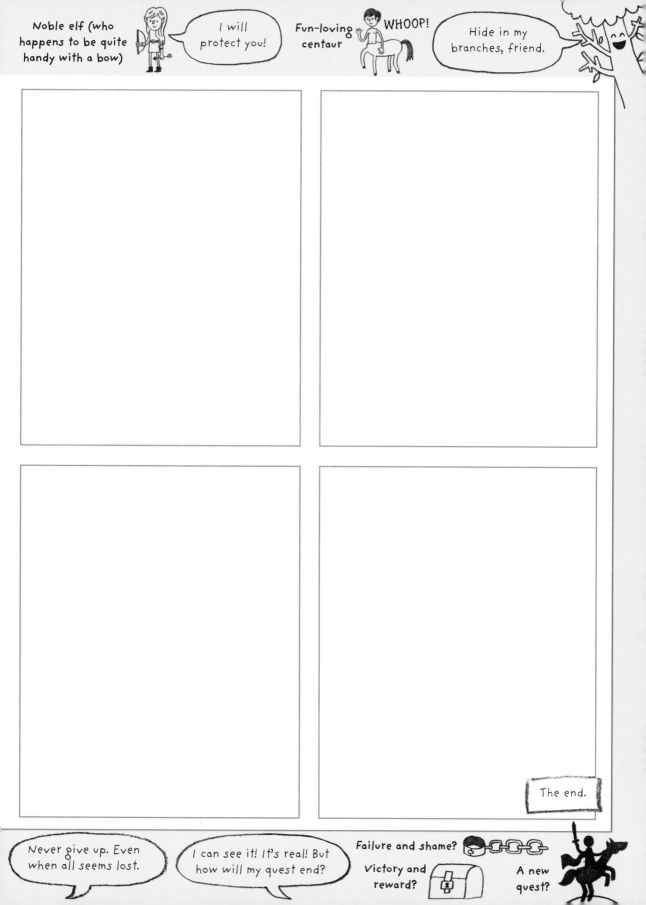

Noble elf (who happens to be quite handy with a bow)

I will protect you!

Fun-loving centaur

WHOOP!

Hide in my branches, friend.

The end.

Never give up. Even when all seems lost.

I can see it! It's real! But how will my quest end?

Failure and shame?

Victory and reward?

A new quest?

How to be a cat

Title?

How does the day start at kitten school?

Some poses

Sitting

Standing

Sleeping

Running

Continued ➡

Kitten faces

Stripes

Smudgy spots

Really big eyes

What are the classrooms like at kitten school?
Do they have any classes outdoors?

Panel ideas

To show the teacher talking to the class, you could draw it like this.

To draw lots of kitties talking together, try this.

SIT DOWN!

If the teacher gets angry and shouts, you could write his or her speech in big letters.

What might make a cat teacher angry?

Steam

Watching videos of humans on Mewtube in class

Not sharing your toys

Claiming the dog ate your homework

What experiments might kittens do in a science class?
What songs would they sing in kitten choir?

YOWL!

Continued →

What might make a cat teacher happy?

A++

Getting the top grade in a Pouncing exam

Putting your paw up before you meow

A present for teacher

How does the school day end?
What do the kittens do for fun after school?

The end.

SCRATCH!   MEEP!   PURRRRRRRR!

Time travel

Title?

Who are your time tourists?

Reasons for time travel

To meet famous people?

To change history?

TITANIC

Don't get on! It's going to sink!

To explore the future?

Continued ➡

87

Do your characters get into any trouble?
How is life different in the past or future?

Historical
characters   Musketeers   En garde!   Old-fashioned   European
                                          fighting talk   royalty

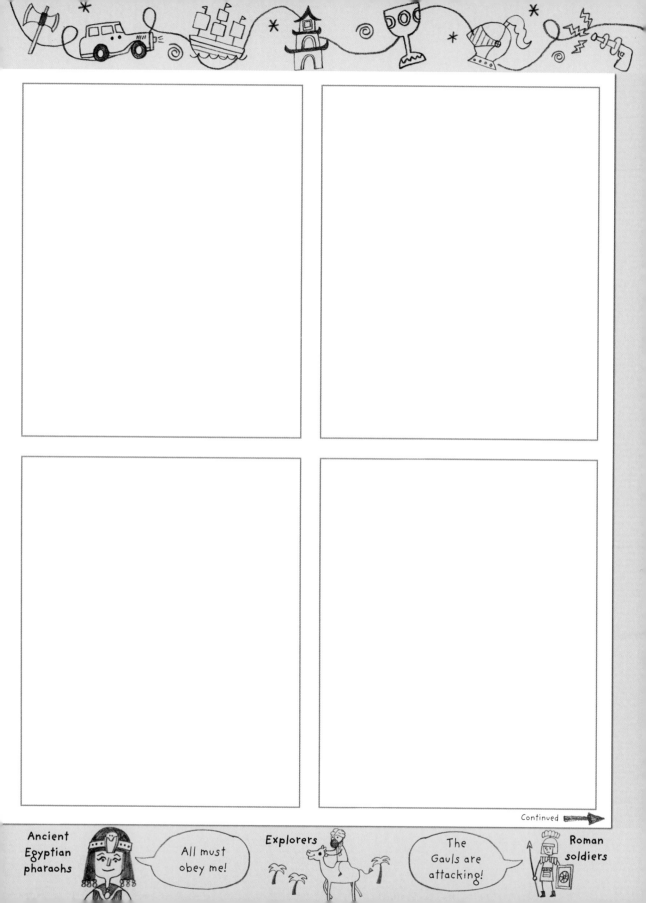

Continued ➤

Ancient Egyptian pharaohs

All must obey me!

Explorers

The Gauls are attacking!

Roman soldiers

Perhaps something goes wrong... your explorers make a mistake, or the time machine breaks?

fZZZZZzzt!

KABLOOEY!

Time travel trouble

Old-fashioned diseases

Finding yourself in the middle of a brutal war

Time machine breakdown

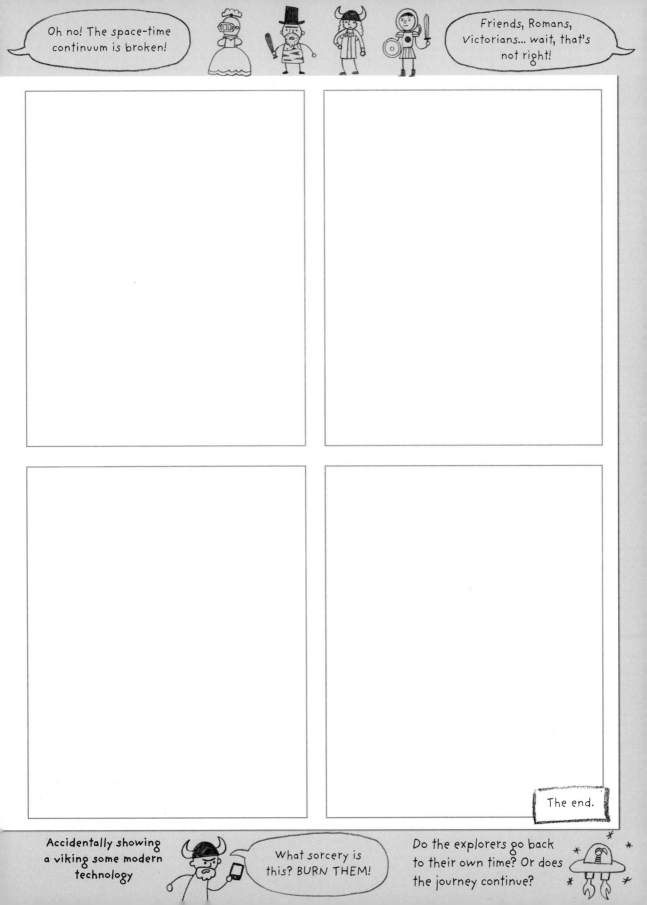

Drawing covers

The cover of a comic has to grab your reader's attention and show what the story is about.

Here are a few covers for different types of stories.

The title is usually nice and big — easy to read from a distance.

The title could go on more than one line.

A tag line like this can help lure readers in.

You could draw a very bold cover, without much detail, just shapes and outlines.

Don't forget to leave room for your name somewhere. Comics that are by two people usually just have their last names on the cover.

Draw a cover for one of the comics you've made in this
book — or for a comic that you'd love to write one day.

A few last tips

The more comic strips you write and draw, the better you get. So make comics whenever you can.

SCRIBBLE

THE WORLD HAS NEVER SEEN SUCH BRILLIANCE.

← AMAZING

← BETTER

← GOOD

← OK

Draw people and objects you see when you're out and about.

SKETCH SKETCH

Keep a book of doodles and random ideas...

...you never know when you might accidentally create a character.

I'm Mr. Stinky the Dung Beetle.

Try making collage comics.

Collage using scrap paper

← Drawn-on face and other details

Try silent comics...

The pictures can tell a story on their own, without any words.

Who did what in this book?

The amazing art is by...

Jess Bradley

Neill Cameron

Freya Harrison

Laura Howell

Adam Larkum

Igor Sinkovec

You

Words by me.

Louie Stowell

Edited by me.

Ruth Brocklehurst

Designed by me.

Russell Punter

Our expert comics and literacy consultants were...

Dr. Matt Finch

Dr. Kerenza Ghosh

Usborne Quicklinks

For links to websites where you can find out more about writing and drawing your own comic strips, go to usborne.com/Quicklinks and type in the title of this book.

Children should be supervised online. Please follow the internet safety guidelines at Usborne Quicklinks.

First published in 2014 by Usborne Publishing Limited, 83-85 Saffron Hill, London EC1N 8RT, United Kingdom. usborne.com

Copyright © 2014, 2024 Usborne Publishing Limited. All rights reserved. No part of this publication may be reproduced, stored in a retrieval system or transmitted in any form or by any means without the prior permission of the publisher. The name Usborne and the balloon logo are registered trade marks of Usborne Publishing Limited. First published in America in 2015. This edition published in 2024. UE

Usborne Publishing is not responsible for the content or availability of any website other than its own.